NEVER
TOO LATE

LIFE INTERRUPTED BY THE SUPERNATURAL

BY K.K. MAC

PUBLISHED BY

WORD PRODUCTIONS

NEVER
TOO LATE

LIFE INTERRUPTED BY THE SUPERNATURAL

BY K.K. MAC

To Contact the Ministry Email:

Chatwithkaykaymac@gmail.com

PUBLISHED BY

WORD PRODUCTIONS

Published by
WORD PRODUCTIONS LLC

Never Too Late: Life Interrupted by the Supernatural
By K. K. Mac

Copyright © 2018
By K. K. Mac

ISBN: 978-0-9978373-4-6

All rights reserved. Under International Copyright Law, no part of this publication may be reproduced, stored, or transmitted by any means—electronic, mechanical, photographic (photocopy), recording, or otherwise—without written permission from the Publisher. Printed in the United States of America.

All Scripture taken from the New King James Version, Copyright ©1982 by Thomas Nelson, Inc., unless otherwise noted.
Used by permission. All rights reserved.

DEDICATION

For...

Scott

David

Jesse

"These are my sons in whom I am well pleased!"

...and Stacy

My very bestest friend ever...in the whole world!

...Four of the greatest gifts that God has graced my life with!

INTRODUCTION

Create in me a clean heart, O God, and renew a steadfast spirit within me. —Psalm 51:10

I HAVE EXPERIENCED MUCH DERISION FROM sharing these stories with family and friends. These are not stories but very true to my life encounters with history, God and the supernatural. Many speculate that I must have been dreaming or been in some drug induced state, or that it is a fictitious imagination or an allegory to promote spiritualism propaganda. None of these are true. What is true is that these experiences really happened and that I'm writing it exactly how I remember it. My hope in writing this is to convey to the reader that I must simply be faithful to what I have been entrusted with in the hope that it may stir your faith-journey as it has radically stirred mine.

My earliest awareness of God was when I was about five or six years old. I found that I could sing. Hidden in my way too fast vibrato was untapped potential that my Dad recognized and started having me perform at birthday parties, political socials and public events. It was something that I really enjoyed as a small child so when asked, "Where did you get that voice?", I simply replied that God must have given it to me. So with strong resolve and certitude that this was indeed something that God gifted me with, I embarked on a career in singing that took me thru several genres of music like Spanish, Folk, Country Western, and now Gospel with countless studio sessions and recordings that has spanned my life even to the present. Never breaking into the national charts my husband reminded me that I woke every morning doing the very thing that I was created to be and that God didn't measure success like Billboard Magazine.

Then about nine or ten years old, I was taught in my religion class that we were to go to confession every Saturday so on my way to the confessional one morning I was debating with myself if I even had a sin that I could confess to the awaiting priest. I entered the booth and said from memory," Forgive me father, it has been a week since my last confession." He said a blessing over me and then asked what sin(s) I needed to be absolved from. Trying hard to raise up any hidden sin, he startled me with his impatient raised voice and repeated himself but before he could finish, I lied and made up that I had yelled at my mom. With ten hail Mary's to recite for my penance I quickly exited the booth to a nearby pew. Bothered by the fact that I had just lied in the confessional I had an epiphany that I would never again confess to any-man but only to God from now on. This emboldened stance that I took as a child, has opened constant discourse between God and myself that has piqued my curiosity to better know Him and better still, learn all about His beloved Son.

If asked what one thing could I describe my relationship with God through the years, I could not because there are so many facets of His Divine Self. When I was a child, I received a gift of a kaleidoscope. Made of tin and cardboard from the five and dime store, it became one of my favorite pastimes. I'd spend hours looking through amazed that I could never find the same pattern, each one became my favorite. Later when it was old and broken, I took it apart to see that it was only bits of pretty colored shards of glass and mirrors. Similarly my life had many broken pieces of pretty glass along my journey. But when I looked at them with the same perception as God, using mirrors to reflect His glory, it became a work of art.

Another revelation perspective is that He wants us to know who we are. Our identity with Christ is paramount. We are more than just human. It is no longer I who live but Christ in me. Gal 2:20. For in Him we live and move and have our being. Acts 17:28. Meditating daily on scripture like these has challenged my faith to believe what God says about me. I am not who I think I am, I am who God says I am.

Another perspective, and probably for me the most poignant, is that I have become the object of His affection. Every path of my long journey has been blanketed by His immutable love. He called me beloved and wrote my name in the palm of His hand, Isaiah 49:16, so I ran to get a tattoo on the inside of my left wrist that reads 'Beloved'. I want to rise every morning reminding me of who I am. I am His beloved and He is mine. One of my favorite poems written reads:

The Object of His Love
A poem by Stacy McDermott

Before there was a universe for You to hang the stars;
Before You had created time with years and days and hours;
Before created angels stood to worship at Your Throne;
God of Love, Sweet Three in One, You must have felt alone.

Before any created thing by Your first Word began;
You always were. No start no end, eternally I Am.
When suddenly from deep within, the revelation sprang;
A counterpart for You to Love, and You would call him "man."

And so began Your romance, now at last You'd have a bride;
An object of Your Love so deep, who'd carry Your own life.
So from Your Word, the light burst forth;
The stars and planets on their course.
And on the day before Your rest,
You fashioned from created earth,
The object of Your Love and Faith.
A man now filled with Your own breath
And clothed with your own Glory;

And then Your image opened eyes;
Beheld Your beauty and Your Grace.
Before a tick of time could pass,
You first found Love returned at last!

In Zephaniah 3:17, it says that God rejoices over us with singing. It's true, but His choice of songs may surprise and delight you.

Not too long ago I awoke to someone singing an old Buck Owens tune called, "I've Got a Never Ending Love for You!" I turned to see if it could be my husband, but he was still fast asleep. I looked over at my dog and she too was lost in slumber. I just laid back in delight believing that it was my Father's good morning kiss.

Even through the tragedies of life, nothing can separate me from His Love...nothing. The apostle Paul says in Phillipians 3:10 AMP, that it was his determined purpose to know Christ more deeply, and intimately...recognizing and understanding the wonders of His Person more strongly and clearly.

This has become my daily prayer now, because as I come to know Him intimately, I come to know myself. I want to walk with Him in my dreams or perhaps His. He has truly become the "lover of my soul," and He is calling all of His created children to Himself to shower you in His infinite Love so that you will find your completeness in Him.

My sincerest hope in writing these pages is that you will answer His invitation to His welcome home party and become everything that He has made you to be, remembering that for you, He is NEVER TOO LATE!

CONTENTS

1

SUPERNATURAL VISITATION
2000 YEARS AGO

*"And it shall be in the last days," God says, " that I will
pour forth of My Spirit upon all mankind; and your sons
and your daughters shall prophesy, and your young men
shall see visions and your old men shall dream dreams;
Even upon my bondslaves, both men and women, I will in
those days pour forth of My Spirit and they shall prophesy."*
—*Acts 2:17-18.*

I DON'T WANT TO BORE YOU WITH my religious upbringing or
bring indictment to any one denomination. Suffice it to say, at
nineteen years old I was pleased and comfortable with my pseudo-
relationship with the heavenlies.

I believed in God the Father, His son Jesus, and the Holy
Spirit, but kept them at arms length—except when I needed to
make an emergency withdrawal. I observed every holy day on the

calendar as well as most Sundays to try and fulfill my obligations. I was pretty sure that I was pleasing to God because I was forever trying to be a "good" person.

I was home fixing lunch for my roommate and myself when there was an unexpected knock on our door. It was my roommate's brother, Don, bearing gifts, smoked BBQ sandwiches from our favorite eatery just around the corner.

We had just finished feasting when I noticed Don nervously clearing his throat. "I want to tell you that Jesus wants you to be *born again!* He continued talking but my mind went back to high school to a moment when I had reluctantly accepted a dinner date with a classmate that I didn't know very well. Instead of dinner or a movie, we ended up in this church of an unfamiliar denomination and unfamiliar people. We listened to someone speak for forty-five minutes or so. I was only half listening because I was feeling angry and very hungry. The speaker finished his half-heard speech and then asked the congregation to come up to the altar and get "born-again." This was a term I had never heard.

I was glad to get ready to leave, when my date ran to the altar and was then escorted through an auspicious door. He left me! Was he coming back? Were we still going to dinner? After what seemed about twenty minutes or so with no sign of life at that altar, I collected my things and walked home. Needless to say, me and "born-again" were not on good terms.

So now, with my attention back at home, I suddenly stood in defiance to express my litany of reasons why I didn't want to go down that same bunny trail when something very unexpected happened.

Somehow, swept away from my living room, I found myself out on a desert-like scape. There was a strong wind blowing dust all around that blurred my vision. Just ahead, I could barely make out the shape of a telephone pole or a tree. I was confused and a little scared about the transition that just took place from my home to a desert...this was all quite disconcerting. In my vision, I pushed on through the dust and heavy wind toward the pole so I could try to gain some perspective of where I was. Finally reaching the pole, it felt more like a railroad timber sticking straight up from the ground. Still, because of the blowing dust, I could see nothing.

A soft murmur of human voices started to swell in a circle around the pole and me. As they got louder, I could hear some soft whimpering along with mixed voices—some talking, some jeering, and even some laughter. With still no visual, the voices started mocking and jeering at a volume that I could now plainly hear. I distinctly heard a loud voice say: "If you are the Son of God, why don't you come down from there?"

Where was I? What was going on? My flurried thoughts took me back to when I had heard many sermons in church about the crucifixion of Jesus. This scenario was placing me right smack in the middle of that holy scene on Calvary. I grabbed on tighter to that hand-hewn piece of wood and started following it slowly, up, up, up. I never saw the people who belonged to the voices but as the dust cleared around the pole, I saw Him! I saw Jesus! He was hanging from the same pole that I was hanging on to. His eyes were shut like you would see someone wincing in pain. Drenched in blood that was still dripping, I heard Him whimper.

Filled with despair, I called out to Him, "Please Jesus, is this really necessary? I don't understand. Do you really have to do this for these wicked sinners?" Suddenly, it was as if my own words were melding with the surrounding voices that were still mocking Him from the unseen crowd. Feeling remorseful for sounding just like them, I cried out once again, "Please Jesus, do you have to do this for them?"

Jesus opened his eyes and looked straight into mine. And the words He spoke shook me from the molecular depths of my being. He said, "I have to, I have to do this for Kay Kay!" His words slew me as if a great giant sword severed me in halves. I fell to the ground shamed and disgusted at myself to even be in the vicinity of this Holy God. I cried out to Him to just destroy me, for I could now feel the unbearable weight of my sin and smell the filth of my flesh. "Destroy me," I pleaded again, as I could no longer look upon Him.

I can only describe what happened next as a feeling of warm sunlight that fell on my head and then slowly encased me in what seemed like a bubble of warm oil mixed with furious white-hot love. It was a feeling something like a fetus secure in its mother's womb.

I suddenly appeared back home but sprawled on the floor in a puddle of tears and slobber. My roommate was trying to lift me to my feet and asked, "What are you doing?" I tried to explain with my choked up reply, "Didn't you see? Didn't you hear?" With blank looks they hurried out the door with plans and excuses. I didn't mind, for it gave me time to revel in this new feeling or new someone that was sitting in my living room.

This encounter changed me from my spiritual core. I started devouring the Bible and book-after-book to discover clues to answer my many questions. I found destiny and purpose and direction for my life. I had been showered in forgiveness, drowned in His immutable love. I was born anew…or again. It was also interesting that Jesus spoke my nickname. Not the name that is on my birth certificate or the one that solicitors call me. He spoke the name that only those that know me well or are on a friendly basis use.

A few years later I met a beautiful man. Like me, he was a musician. We fell in love with Jesus, and then with each other. We married and swiftly started a Word and worship ministry called Holy Smoke. The ministry became a whirlwind of evangelistic travel across the U.S. and then abroad, preaching God's goodness and singing His praises. After seven or eight years we were called to pastor a small church in Albuquerque, New Mexico, called Worldwide Worship Center.

In our mid-sixties now, we have been pastors and evangelists for 36 years with no plans to ever retire from ministry.

This is how my great adventure began with the Holy Spirit—an adventure that has continued throughout the decades and I pray will continue to my last breath.

ANGELS, ANGELS, ANGELS!

Angels watching over Me
Every step I take
Every move I make.
Angels watching over me.
(From the song by Amy Grant)

LIKE US, ANGELS COME IN ALL SHAPES and sizes, dress codes, and in every kind of work place. We were living in Las Vegas, Nevada, and attending an Evangelistic Training Center and working at a school of reformation for young boys.

I was going to have some time off and really wanted to visit my parents who were living in Phoenix, Arizona. It was not too far away. My husband drove me to the airport so I could catch a short flight to visit my parents for a few days. I was looking forward to spending time with them and getting some much-needed rest.

On the last day of my short but very sweet visit with my parents, my father asked me what time I needed to be at the airport to catch my flight. I told him 5pm. It was just that time when we rolled up to the curb at the airport for departures. I grabbed my small suitcase, kissed my daddy goodbye, and hurried toward my gate.

Ticket in hand, I glanced at it to see which gate I was departing from when I realized that it said departure was at 5:00!

I made a mad dash through the Phoenix airport to catch my plane. As I approached the gate, I noticed it was completely empty. There was no one in sight, and I could see my plane rolling down the tarmac.

With not a human in sight at the gate, I reread the fine print on my ticket: "No refunds, no returns!" I whipped around to rethink how I could get back home.

I looked to find a seat so I could sit down for a moment to recover from feeling stupid, when I literally slammed into a man wearing a pilot's uniform with gold stripes on his sleeves and a pilot's cap.

He interrupted me as I was profusely apologizing for not looking where I was going. He began, "Missed your flight, didn't you?"

"Well yes!" I said."

"Come with me over to the counter and I'll take care of that for you."

I followed him over to the nearest ticket counter and he started typing on the computer. I noticed that there was still not a person in sight in all of the departing gates in that cul-de-sac. I told him what my ticket said about missed flights and he said not to worry as he continued typing. "Well it looks like I can get you on the very next flight departing in 45 minutes," he said.

"Oh yes, thank you," I said. I was so relieved that I could still make it home that night. I suddenly remebered that my husband was waiting for me in the Las Vegas airport!

Without an interruption in his typing, he said, "You have someone waiting for you on that flight don't you?"

I was astonished that he even thought about that and that he even cared. I started sensing something was up. Then he said, "Let's just call the airport and page your husband so you can tell him about your delay." So he turned to a wall phone and dialed the Las Vegas Airport for me and told me to ask the operator to page my husband. He continued typing while the phone was ringing.

Readying myself to speak to the operator, it rang, rang again, then once more when suddenly a voice answered, "Hello?" It was *not* the voice of the airport operator. It was my husband's voice.

"How in the world am I speaking with you," I asked, "The pilot dialed the page operator at the airport." I glanced over to the pilot who was still typing behind the counter. My husband said that he was just walking down the hall toward my arriving gate when a phone on the wall started ringing and he just answered it. This was just too much! I explained how I had missed my flight and I would be on the very next flight. He said no worries because he would sit at the nickle machines during the interim.

Still in shock that all this could happen, I returned the phone back to the pilot. He was still typing but I knew that he could hear my remarkable telephone conversation. I felt that he must be my guardian angel so I started intensely looking at his pilot uniform to look for some sure signs of wings or feathers. Suddenly he looked up from his typing and looked right at me. I fessed up and told him that I was sure that he was an angel and that I was looking for wings or something. He smiled and confidently told me that he did have wings.

I was so excited, I thought he was going to shed his human facade and unfurl his feathery wings when he pointed to the shiny metal wings on his uniform. Somewhat disappointed but still reeling with all that had just happened, I started thanking him for all that he had done for me.

Still expressing my gratefulness to him, I bent down to pick up my suitcase. I then stood back up to say my final goodbye to my new pilot friend, but he was gone. He was nowhere in sight. I walked around to the other side of the counter to look for him. He had vanished. No sound, no flash, and no more typing.

I sat down on the nearest seat to wait for my flight...delighting in the fact that I had had an angelic encounter made the time fly by. Finally, people started walking back into the area to find seats to wait for their departing flights, while I was still wondering if time had stopped for me and my angelic pilot friend in order for us to figure out a way for me to get home.

"Then I saw another angel flying in the midst of heaven, having the everlasting gospel to preach to those who dwell on the earth." —Rev 14:6

This next angel doesn't come into this story until the very end but here is how it started:

My husband and I were invited to be on a ministry team that traveled to South America. It was my first trip there so I was excited to be a part of God's ministry plans. Once there, we were split up to stay at different people's houses as there were about fifteen of us on the team. We stayed with a lovely mother and her two young daughters. We could tell that they had prepared their nicest room to be our sleeping quarters with netting over the bed to dissuade mosquitos, two fans to keep the room cool at night, and fresh clean-smelling bedding. We enjoyed a meal together getting to know our hosts and then settled down for the night after a long flight from Miami. Comfortable and secure, we drifted off into a deep slumber. However, only hours later I awoke with a start. Something was wrong. I couldn't catch my breath. I stole away trying not to wake my husband while tiptoeing to the living quarters and settling in a chair to try again to take deep breaths. It wasn't working so I started to pray and ask for God's help because this was the first day of a two-week ministry engagement.

Morning came at a snail's crawl but I was glad to see the sun while hoping that this ordeal would soon be over. I hurried back to our bedroom where my husband was just waking and told him of my problem. His first thought was that I needed to acclimate to the below sea-level air. Breathe into a bag was his advice. So after waiting to hear kitchen noise, I ventured into the kitchen to ask our host if she had a bag that I could use. I couldn't bring myself to eat so I passed on the lovely breakfast that she had prepared filled with indigenous fruits, cheeses, and sausages.

Our team came together somewhere in a downtown public building where I was able to find the doctor that was part of our ministry team. I rushed to tell him that I was having great trouble breathing. He told me that I was just acclimating to the area and that it would soon go away and to keep breathing in my paper bag. Sorely disappointed that he could do no more for me, I did all that they told me but I could tell it was getting worse. I felt that with each exhale my lungs were being squeezed tighter and tighter so that when I inhaled, it was only in very short pants. I remember my biology teacher in high school saying that if your blood is not oxygenated properly it will look black so I punctured my little finger with a fork and only little black dots surfaced. I had to focus on ministering to these people so when we got up to sing our worship songs, I found some breath. It seemed easier. But as soon as we stopped, the short panting started again. What was this? What is wrong with me? God, please help me.

Hours turned into days and as they passed no one seemed to notice that I was struggling because each time we sang, I was able to somehow take breath. I continued to pass on every meal because I didn't want to obstruct the only air passage I had with food. Nights grew into sleepless nightmares of trying to breathe and praying no-faith prayers. More days passed and I was getting weaker with no food and little water, no sleep, and no breath. About the seventh day I remember barely getting up to sing with the little strength I had left when a very strange sensation swept over me. It was a deep darkness that I had never known before but it lifted as I started to sing. This time I knew that I was somehow caught in a spiritual battle but I had not the strength to fight. That night I asked my husband to read from the bible to calm my fears but he fell into deep sleep midsentence because I had been keeping him awake with my torment.

It was then that I reached for the phone to call my friend back in the states. She was watching our boys for us while we were in South America. She immediately knew that something was wrong so I asked to speak to my boys. The only one home was the smallest so I asked him if he could see the moon. He said, "Yes." I told him that I could see the moon from where I was, too, and that we can connect looking at the same moon even though we were so far apart. Saying goodbye to my baby somehow felt so final. I knew that I didn't have the strength to continue on anymore so I prayed a prayer to commend myself into God's hands, closed my eyes, and passed out.

In the morning I awoke very surprised! Surprised that I woke up number one, and two, surprised that I could breathe better. We had such a harried schedule ministering morning, noon, and night. I remember getting ready to sing with our trio when that same dark dread tried to overwhelm me, but this time it seemed to pass through me with no power. I felt a little stronger now but somehow I knew this battle wasn't over. Still not able to eat, drink, or sleep after eight days into our trip, I finally broke down into a crying, slobbery mess in the middle of a hotel lobby. Now getting the attention of some of the other team members, my friend, the evangelist, came over to see me. Right there in the lobby, he and my husband prayed out loud for me until I suddenly gasped and took in a huge breath of fresh air. It felt like a very tight belt around my core had broken and fallen away. It felt so good that I took another and then another.

I could breathe normally again but to make sure, I asked my escorts to walk with me outside awhile. I started to jog, I felt so good. Suddenly I felt the pangs of hunger and I said, "Lets go eat!" So I joined the whole team this time in a meal and celebration of my conversion from the walking dead. In a more sober tone, my friend leaned over to tell me that he felt that this was not yet over. Not what I wanted to hear so I shelved it not to think of it again. Growing stronger everyday, we finished our two week ministry opportunity and on the last day as we were packing getting ready to go, I heard someone say, "You'll never come back!" I don't know if I heard it with my ears or my head or what but that same dark dread accompanied the voice.

Back at home about four months later, I had caught a very bad cold and was coughing, sneezing, and trying to breathe through my mouth. It was time to turn in so I told my husband to go on ahead to bed and that I would stay on the couch so that I wouldn't keep him awake. After transforming our couch into a somewhat comfortable bed, I tried to settle in but became restless with a bad feeling of an old familiar darkness and dread that threatened to overwhelm me.

As I lay there wide awake and propped up with pillows, I noticed that the ceiling and roof of my house had disappeared. Just the blackness of sky dotted with the bright stars shone down on me. No sound, no wind, but from the corner of the sky I could make out an even brighter star moving across, what used to be, my ceiling growing closer and closer. It stopped right above me and through its brilliance, I could see a huge, just humongous angelic being. He must have been 4 to 5 stories tall, wearing a brilliant white robe cinched at the waist. He had flowing hair and beautiful feather wings as long as he was. With his right foot, he took a running start and kicked something from out of the darkness that I could feel but not see. The angel kicked it so hard that it shot into the dark sky making a horrid shriek as it vanished into the cosmos.

He turned to go but then said, "Oh Yah," and with his left arm, he reached into my home with his very big hand and tweaked my nose. And with that he turned and jetted off into the starry sky. In an instant, I was changed. No more coughing, no more sneezing, and I was now able to breathe freely through my nose. After watching my roof and then my ceiling coming back into view, I jumped off the couch and started screaming, Thank you!" to my now far away angelic friend. Waking my husband with my excitement, he asked me what was going on. I told him everything that happened and after some time of rejoicing, we left the couch to go back to bed.

It has been decades and that dark dread has never returned. And as it turned out, we did go back. Our ministry team returned seven more times, over and over to share the goodness of God. I became fearless, never afraid to minister wherever He sends me. I now live with the certitude that I am surely never alone and He always has my back.

"Then an angel passed before my face; the hair on my body stood up..." —Job 4:15

This next angelic visit happened in October 2014, not to or for me, but I was elated to be a witness to someone else's experience.

In our small church, we have many ordained ministers who have community outreaches. This particular outreach is called, "Christian Rods and Customs." This ministry is headed by one of our congregants named Ken who is their regional president.

They have many car shows all over the state that culminate at the huge state fair, called "Supernationals," in February every year. Also, in the fall, when the leaves start to turn, they have a yearly, "Tour de Northern New Mexico." This is a convoy of car members who travel from Rio Rancho up through the beautiful Jemez Mountains. These mountains are filled with gorgeous scenery like the Valle Grande, teaming with elk and sites like drive-through natural tunnels. Then gorgeous sunlit colors of autumn lead you through the winding road toward Los Alamos. After filling up on Indian fry bread and local honey and gasoline, we trek on northward to the little village of Chimayo where we scout more local artisans and craft vendors. We end up at a lovely authentic Chimayo restaurant to swap exciting stories and show our treasures.

As we were climbing the winding road through the Jemez, still quite a ways from Los Alamos, one of the cars in the convoy started breaking down. The convoy pulled over to the side to determine what to do next. This car was a 1948 Chevy, that belonged to a lovely couple who had been a part of CR and C (the group) for many years. After some time under the car, they determined that the shock bolt had snapped and broken and that the car would have to be towed.

They now had to decide to leave their car and go to the nearest town to hire a tow truck and they had no idea what to do. The entire convoy had pulled over to the side of the road waiting on what options our friends would choose.

Suddenly, a truck that was passing by pulled over to see what was going on. The driver was a young man in his early twenties or so. He wore a blue and white flannel shirt with blue jeans and had dark hair. He wanted to know what was going on and if he could help. When they told him that the shock bolt of their '48 Chevy snapped and broke off somewhere, he smiled and said that he just happened to have one of those in the bed of his truck and that it *just so happened* he had the right tool to replace it.

In total amazement, we watched as this young man got under their car, fixing the problem like he was being timed on a calf-roping contest. After waiving goodbye, he jumped back in his truck and drove off.

When we finally got to the restaurant in Chimayo, there was a lot of celebrating and discussion about how our "mechanic angel friend" had saved the day. We rejoiced in knowing that there are, most definitely, "Angels watching over us!"

GOING SOUTH
ON MOTHER'S DAY

ONE MOTHER'S DAY, OUR MINISTRY team of four was invited to minister at a non-denominational church about four hours south of Albuquerque. Our day started off early so we could get on the road. Our team consisted of my husband, Stacy, our best friends, Mimi and her husband JC, and then myself.

Stacy, Mimi, and I would begin each of our services with prayer and then worshipful music. We had learned years ago that this part of the service was God's favorite because He already knew His Word. The sermons were for encouragement and building up of the congregation. JC did this so well, teaching and preaching of the goodness of God.

We had just started the last song when I noticed a small fly buzzing around the stage. I repeatedly shooed it away as it came near me several times...and too close for comfort. Then I had the thought that the people couldn't see the small fly and that I probably looked like I was having a seizure so I told myself to just relax, that it would go away and that I should concentrate on my worship of God. Well that didn't happen because when I drew my next breath, that fly was on its way down my throat.

Knowing that flies are probably the most filthy, I tried to cough it back out. But when I looked in my hand to see if it worked, I only found an unattached fly wing. I was so grossed out that I ran to the pulpit in front of Stacy, shoved him aside and started searching for water. Stacy and Mimi continued on singing not aware of what was transpiring.

Making a mess of the inside of the pulpit, I finally found a half empty bottle of water. I knew the fly wasn't coming up, so now it was going down. Still coughing with water dripping down my face, I now realized that I had a fly corpse in my gut, which made my stomach feel like it was turning inside out. I was trying my best to hold back a spectacular vomit on stage.

With Stacy and Mimi still having their eyes closed, not missing a beat, I ran off the stage to the nearest bathroom. After hugging a public toilet trying my best not to sound like a foghorn, I finally came out of the bathroom.

Service had ended so I immediately ran to the van to look for some crackers to calm my unrelenting very upset stomach when I noticed a young boy following me. At the van he caught up with me. He tugged on my skirt and asked me what the heck was going on with me up there?

Still very frazzled with my experience, I replied with a not so Christian response, "Nothin! Go on, get outta here!"

The ride home seemed like eight hours instead of four. I just wanted to get home, throw up again, and then soak my memories away in a warm tub trying to forget my harried Mother's Day. I had plenty of time to think about this on the road home and finally squeezed something good out of this experience and that was that now I can say...

"Don't mess with me, cuz this mama eats flies!"

4

CHAPTER

MY HOSPITAL VISIT

I AWOKE ONE MORNING WITH A SPLITTING HEADACHE. This was unusual for me as I had never had migraines or frequent headaches. After taking my extremely high temperature, I reached for the phone to call my best friend, who, by the way, was a registered nurse. I asked her what the heck I had. After a few more medical questions, my nose erupted into a cascade of blood flowing down my cheeks. She told me to have my husband rush me to the emergency room and that she would meet me there.

Not even at the hospital yet, I couldn't open my eyes. The daylight only seemed to exacerbate my now growing and excruciating pain. Rushed in for examination, I noticed that I was slurring my speech when answering their questions. I just begged them to "drill a hole in my forehead to let out the fire I was sure was inside."

I don't remember what happened next! I passed out from pain, medication or both. What I do remember is that my whole body was totally paralyzed trying to fight for my consciousness. Trying to push through the murky fog. I could sense someone moving around me.

Still paralyzed, I could tell that I was about to vomit while laying flat on my back. Someone's gentle hands turned my face every time into what I thought was a tray so that I wouldn't asphyxiate. Assured that someone was watching over me, I drifted into a deep dark place. About three days later, I opened my eyes. I had no more pain so I started a panoramic view of my hospital room to assess my environment when my eyes fell upon my sweet RN friend, fast asleep, sitting at my bedside. She didn't even work at that hospital but took off work to watch over me, never leaving my side. I learned later that the nurses came in every fifteen minutes to administer my medication but they had other patients and left the room not knowing that each time it made me regurgitate. It was the gentle hands of my RN friend that would rescue me from asphyxiation, every fifteen minutes, for three days of coma.

She confessed that she was worried for me because the doctors told her that I had contracted *spinal meningitis* and that usually people don't survive it or, if they do, they have different degrees of brain damage. Immediately I recited a poem by John Donne called, "For Whom The Bell Tolls," that I had learned in high school. We both erupted in laughter. Just then someone on staff ran in looking like an asbestos hazmat person, to throw some paperwork on the table and turn to zip out the doors just as fast. Erupting in more laughter, I enjoyed our uninterrupted time with my best friend and now "super hero." As she was getting ready to leave for much needed rest and sleep, I assured her not to worry because there was definitely "still more candy in this piñata."

NOT DUCK...DUCK!

MANY YEARS AGO, I GAVE BIRTH TO A bouncing baby boy we named Scott. He was a good baby. I still commuted out of town for work, so my mother watched him during the day. I received a very upsetting phone call from my mother one day! Scott had developed a high fever. I told her to take him to emergency and that it would take me awhile but that I would meet her there. Later that evening I broke through the emergency doors trying to find what bed they had put my son in, when two nurses took me to the side to explain to me that my son had contracted whooping cough and that his fever had gotten extremely high but that they were able to break it. He was admitted overnight for resting and more examination and with his crib tented so he could get better oxygen.

Filled with mother's anxiety and remorse, I tiptoed over to his crib expecting to see my little boy sick and exhausted but as I drew close, I found Scotty blowing through the oxygen hose like a trumpet. He was sitting up and laughing, assuaging all my fears. He grew into a healthy, sweet, five year old boy.

As he grew older, I started noticing that Scott would ignore me from time-to-time. He wouldn't pick up his toys when I asked or turn from the TV when I spoke to him. Out of frustration, I spanked his little fanny to get him to respond.

It was soon time to get Scott ready for first grade. They scheduled us for his hearing and eye test. The hearing examiner took Scott in by himself and I was told to wait in the hall. Not long afterward I was asked to join my son and the examiner in his office. The examiner showed me plainly on his charts how Scott was deaf to higher decibels and could only make out certain low registers.

This information threw me into a state of hysterical tears. Tears for the little swats on his butt that he got for not turning off the TV when I asked; tears for the swats he got for not putting away his toys when told. After running for water and tissues, the examiner asked me to calm down and then asked if Scotty had ever had a high fever before.

A new burst of hysteria exploded out from me in self-hatred for being such a horrible Momma. I had to sit in the parking lot just holding and kissing my son and asking him to forgive me because I didn't know and had never put it together.

Not long after, a bird flew into the windowpane of our front room. We all heard it and ran outside to see a little bird in my husband's hand. It looked dead but as my husband prayed over it petting its soft feathers, it sat up in his hand and started to chirp. Our three boys and myself started cheering for his recovery and then Scotty asked, "Momma, is that bird making some kind of noise?"

Scott always struggled with his hearing aides. He felt different from his friends at school. So many times after he would return from school, we found them in his pockets, and this day was no different.

I was sitting in my Bible School class when it was interrupted by a police officer and my husband coming to tell me that our son had been hit by a car. It was "a hit-and-run," but Scott was taken to the hospital with severe injuries. At the hospital, we were placed in the next room from where the doctors were performing triage over Scott.

I could hear a very loud moan from the room. A nurse exited the room to tell us that what we are hearing was not Scott necessarily in pain but in trauma.

We had seconds to tell him that we were there for him and that we loved him so much. I spoke loud in his ear to "look to the cross," and heard behind me a strong, "Amen," before his gurney was pulled away from us and hurried to the operating room.

While in the waiting room I could only pace the floor with my Bible held tight to my core. I was unusually calm and not in fear. I had a peace that passed my understanding. The police officer on the scene came in to explain what had happened:

A young girl driving to her high school didn't see Scott as he stepped off the curb. When she hit him, he was thrown 30 feet.

She only had cleared a small hole to see out of her icy and frosted-over windshield. Afraid, knowing she had hit something, she returned home where her grandfather noticed the blood on the car...and asked her what had happened. Terrified, she said she didn't know but that she hit something. Her Grandfather told her that they had to go back to the scene of the crime and speak with the investigators in order to do the right thing.

When we arrived at the hospital, we were given Scott's clothes and an operating room message: *they had to do a more lengthy exploratory surgery.* We found Scott's hearing aides in his jacket pocket.

Since we wouldn't hear any updates for hours, my husband and I decided to go down to the chapel to pray. We had just finished our simple faith-filled prayer when another family rushed into the chapel. They were crying and pleading God for their son who had a neck injury and was also fighting for his life. So we ministered and prayed with them that God would see them through this. We made our way back up to the surgery waiting room, and just held each other and waited.

The first surgeon came out to report that Scott's spleen had to be sewn up but that the other major organs looked intact but still there was much to mend. So we took that as good news and continued praying for divine healing out of chaos, hope for despair, and light from darkness.

Finally, the team of surgeons came to talk with us and told us that they had to set several broken bones which required casts on his body. His spine looked intact but he would still have to wear the casts for six months. We were still waiting for the results from his skull x-rays; but they had done all that they could do for now. They said that his growth platelets were going to give him problems and prevent him from growing tall, and later in life if he survived, he would walk with a bad limp. They said that they hoped that this would be enough to get him through this trauma but that they could promise nothing.

We were escorted to the ICU floor where Scott was still unconscious. It looked like a scene from horror movie. His extremities were all casted and pulled away from his body hanging from a myriad of chains lifting him with just his core touching the bed. He had tubes going in and out of every orifice and machines of every kind beeping some kind of eerie opus. The imagery was that of a Frankenstein spider caught up in his own web.

After the initial shock of seeing our little boy so helpless, we prayed again for the comfort of His presence to keep going forward for our son's sake. Then a glimmer of real hope came in the room when our son opened his eyes and recognized his mommy and daddy.

He was in the ICU for 3 weeks slowly recovering. He was becoming more and more lucid, but he couldn't remember the accident at all. The nurse on duty gave him a self-medication pump to use for pain when needed.

I stayed with him every day as his Dad had to return to his workplace. Every day he got increasingly better. I read fun stories to him and we played dot-to-dot games. There was no TV in his room so I had to get creative with ways to spend quality time with our son who was exponentially healing.

Later that day, when my husband joined us after work, we were asked to join the nurse in her private office for counsel. *We couldn't believe the strong rebuke that we were hearing.* She was very upset and told us 'how dare we not allow our son to use the pump medication for his pain.'

We told her we had given no such instruction to our son. She ranted again that we had no right to tell him not to use it because of our religion.

We tried to explain that if he needed the pain medication, that he would use it and that we would never keep him from using it, but to no avail. So we left to go back to the ICU and asked Scott if he was not using his medication pump because he thought we didn't want him to and he said, "No, I don't need it because I feel no pain anywhere!"

"All this time?" I asked.

"Yup, I don't have any pain in my whole body!"

We were just as surprised as the nasty nurse that he never used the morphine pump. So with great elation, we celebrated knowing that he had been in better hands all this time.

I wrapped up the chord on our small portable TV to take to the hospital. Setting it up for him in his room was a real treat for him because he loved the show, "Chips." California Highway Interstate Police Something.

Oh well, it was about cops on motorcycles in California. He loved it and it helped with the passing of time. Some of the doctors returned to see and examine Scott. They were all so surprised at his quick recovery. They said he could soon be released, but that they had to put him in a full body cast from his neck down to his ankles and his arms out from their sides.

So, eager to take him home finally, we kissed him goodnight and looked forward to the next morning. On returning, I noticed that his countenance was quite sober.

I asked, "What is the matter?"

He said that he wasn't sure but thought that something on TV blew up in the sky. I turned to see what he was watching and it was news coverage on the explosion of the Space Shuttle Challenger. After realizing the loss of the seven astronauts, it was difficult to hide my tears from my convalescing little boy.

I got a surprising phone call that night. It was the mother of the young girl who had hit our son. Her mother was very concerned about her daughter's physical and mental health. She had stopped eating and couldn't sleep. She couldn't stop crying from the guilt of killing our son.

I told her to tell her daughter that she didn't kill him and that he recovered from all of his injuries. I told her to tell her daughter it was an accident, and that she didn't wake that morning planning to strike a little boy down on his way to school. With much relief and a grateful heart, the mother said goodbye with a huge sigh.

After three weeks of the ICU we were ready to bring our little boy back home. His new body cast that he had to wear for six months now left very little in the transport department. We couldn't fit him in our car so we had to put him head first down in the back of the front seats with his legs spread sticking up out of the windows. His only view was the tops of the trees that we drove by but he said how happy he was to finally be going home.

After six months, and with much love and care from his two other brothers and his Mom and Dad, it was time to cut off his body cast. When his skinny legs were finally exposed, he looked like a relative of the Sasquatch.

He had to relearn to walk but soon became a normal 11 year old. Scott grew without a single problem with his platelets or any kind of a limp. He grew to around six feet tall.

Even with his hearing impairment, he now runs his own recording studio for e-books; married his beautiful wife (who we love dearly); and returned to further his education in architectural drafting. To add to that, he is an incredible lip-reader. Scott is a wonderful healthy man and father of our number one grandson, and greatly loved by those who know him.

P.S. One of my sweetest memories of Scott when he was little was the way that he would pronounce his name. Because of his hearing loss, he heard "Duck" when we called him Scott. When he would meet people and they would ask him his name and he would say "Duck."

They would ask again, "Your name is Duck?"

Scott would reply, "No, not "Duck...Duck."

6

"YEAH, SURE DAVY"

"If ye shall ask anything in My name, I will do it."
—John 14:14

OUR MIDDLE SON WAS CHRISTENED David Joseph, a name chosen by his father, but I called him "Davy" because one of his favorite TV shows was about some dynorama-animatonic children's puppet show with a talking dog and a boy named "Davy." Even at five years old, he always recognized my reference to his favorite show when I spoke his name just like the talking dog, "Hello Daaaaavy."

His next favorite thing was to sneak out to the backyard and turn the water on, holding the hose over his head and let the cool water shower down on himself until he was soaked in water, laughter, and delight.

Just after a yummy breakfast, Scott hurried off to school and Jesse was toted off to grandma's for the day. Still too young for school, Davy stayed with me.

I settled in to plan another fun day with him. We were playing with those little metal cars making imaginary roads and bridges all over the living room floor as if it were the city proper when the phone rang. I jumped up to answer it leaving Davy in his little make-believe car city. I was lost in conversation when Davy tugged on my shorts showing me some pennies that he had found and asked if he could go to the store to buy another little car. Thinking how cute he looked holding up his little hand cupping the few pennies, I replied, "Yeah sure Davy," and went back to my phone conversation.

After hanging up, I noticed an eerie silence so I spent awhile calling to Davy looking under beds and in closets thinking we were playing hide and seek. "Davy, where are you?" I said.

He was nowhere to be found. I ran outside to both front and back yards to examine his favorite places to play.

"Davy, where are you?" I shouted once again.

Now in terror, I ran to each corner of our block screaming, "DAVID." With no one in sight, I had to make it back home in case he was still hiding somewhere. I pounded on my neighbors' doors on the way back home to ask if they had seen David, but no one had.

After more desperate searches through the house and yards, I could no longer fight the impending darkness that flooded my soul or the heart-wrenching, growing agony that my Davy was gone and that I had to somehow call the police and report my Davy as missing.

Crumpled down on the porch steps, weeping uncontrollably in unrelenting growing despair, I waited for my husband and the local Police.

Meanwhile a mile-and-a half down a very busy boulevard, Davy was on his own adventure making his way to the big box store that I had taken him to several times before. He was approaching one of the busiest intersections in town. He had walked all that way somehow by remembering landmarks that looked familiar to him. He just wanted to get to the store to purchase another little car with his shiny pennies...a pretty incredible feat for this little five-year-old.

Coming up to the bustling two lane turn and intersection, he waited for the cars to stop. Suddenly, he stepped down in front of a row of heaving hot motor breath cars—barely able to see over their bumpers, was a little head bobbing along, crossing in front of them. Once he got to the sidewalk, the unrelenting challenge lay again before him to cross the perpendicular bustling boulevard. This time, a little old lady took his hand and helped him cross the second intersection.

After crossing him safely on the other side, she asked him, "Does your mother know where you are?"

He proudly nodded his little head and said, "Yes!" He told her that he had to make sure to ask before leaving. So now he had to traverse a huge parking lot alone to get to the front doors of the box store. But for the grace, mercy, and help from God, Davy entered the store intent on shopping but ended up in a cashier lane. He asked the lady if he could get another car, showing her his copper treasure and she told him that he didn't have enough but that he could buy some gum. So he settled on the gum purchase, popped a piece into his mouth, and exited the store to begin his trek home.

Back at the house, I was slipping fast into an emotional numbing blur that felt like I was an empty shell of a person. Almost robotically, I searched for pictures of Davy to give to the policemen so that they could put out an immediate APB.

Constant "If only I's..." started to haunt my numbing, burning soul like a wicked voice from some horror picture.

"What kind of a mother loses her child in her own home because I hadn't paid attention?"

Interrupting my self-hatred, questions about calling the media outlets so that it would be aired on radio and TV to air that "Albuquerque had another missing child," filled my brain. I pictured emergency lights flashing all around and with the agony of more and more soulish despondency, my knees gave way, and I slipped to the ground.

I could only mouth a simple, silent prayer, "God, please forgive me and bring my Davy back home to me."

I don't know where Davy found the courage to face the high traffic. How did he know what colors of the light to cross or not cross at? How in the world did he recalculate the opposite journey of his trek back home?

Outside again, I somehow walked to the end of our block, away from the reporter's questions and the din that stung my ears. I wanted to take one last look down the empty sidewalk for one more chance of hope.

I stared into the very long distance with a last resolve until I saw a dot. Was it a dot forming over my eyes from staring? Was this the stress of the day?

No! It was moving. The dot seemed to grow with each tick of the clock. Still just a dot, it seemed to be bobbing. With life surging back into my bones and a shot of adrenaline, I bolted down the sidewalk to investigate this perhaps mirage of something or someone.

It was Davy! I could see the outline of his perfect little body. His face was still out of focus but I knew my son. It was Davy! Now closer, I could see the smile on his face as he recognized my voice calling to him.

We fell into each other's arms...me with my surprise, sweat and wonder, and him with a look like he had a story to tell. When we turned the corner, holding each other like the Madonna and child, there came a shout of celebration from the policemen and news reporters and friends that resonated throughout the neighborhood.

After thanking them all for their help, we settled back into our house to feed a hungry household and to listen to all that had happened to Davy on his adventure.

I, as a momma, swore that I would never use the term "yeah sure____" ever again, and I never have.

A hard lesson learned, but I learned that your babies really believe the words that come from your mouth and how important those words are to them.

Today Davy is a grown man married to his wife of dazzling beauty and they have four delectable children. He is a firefighter, singer, songwriter, teacher, and soon to be author.

Funny, but I find myself learning a great deal of God's great immutable love through many of the songs he has written and recorded.

I shudder to think of all the things that could have happened or gone wrong that day, but I revel in the God who heard my desperate cry—the very God who brought my Davy back home to me.

SWEET BABY JESSE

The Spirit of God has made me; the breath of the Almighty gives me life. —Job 33:4

IT IS NOT ALWAYS EASY TO EXPLAIN THE supernatural, but I will do my best to recount an experience I had with the Lord that is as real to me now as it was many years ago. My earnest purpose for this book is to lead you to the truth and Jesus.

Thirty some years ago, in late September, my husband rushed me to the emergency room because of heavy bleeding from my womb. I was three months pregnant and suffering severe cramping. After many x-rays, scans, and questioning, the doctor came to meet and talk with us.

Nothing more could be done to stop the miscarriage, he said, and that I had already miscarried most of the fetus and that there was only little pulp left in my womb. He also wanted to keep me in the hospital overnight to monitor any more bleeding. He said that he would check me in the morning and do a D&C if he needed to.

Two night nurses and my husband rolled my bed into a semi-private room. I was put in the bed closest to the window and another lady patient was already sleeping in the bed closest to the door.

It was about 11pm when my husband bent over to kiss me goodnight. I could see the numbness on his face. The same numbness that was rushing through my veins as reality was raging war with my thoughts.

We were young believers at the time, and our faith in Jesus was growing, but tragedy always has a way of challenging our faith. The nurses and my husband exited quietly, but not before a promise that they would all return at 7am to hear what the doctor would decide.

Only a soft light from the hallway bathed the room. I could still see my sleeping roommate on my right. I was not given any medication because my pain had subsided. There were no slow drips of anything intraveneous; only the slow stream of tears that ran down my cheeks.

Was I responsible somehow for causing the death of my baby? Maybe it was too much exertion from a hike into the mountains, a bumpy car ride, or some unconfessed or hidden sin in my life. I started speaking to my unseen God, and asked him to forgive me for my ambiguous fault that I might be guilty of the loss of my three month unborn baby. I told God that He was too late for this baby but that maybe He would give us another chance one day.

Suddenly the supernatural blanketed the natural when a heavenly downpour caused a great and mighty wind in the hospital room. I looked first toward the window to see if it was open. No, it was shut tight. This wind held me by my core to the bed while everything else seemed to take on a scene like a room tornado.

It was loud like I would expect a tornado to sound like. Then my blankets and my long hair flew up to be a part of the tornado but something still pinned me to my bed.

I screamed to wake my sleeping roommate, "Lady, lady, wake up!" to no avail. How could she not hear the roar of wind in our room? After about what seemed to be a few minutes or so, the tornado wind stopped. My blankets fell back around me, my hair laid back on my pillow and the papers and stuff flying around the room gently eased their way back to their approximate place.

I tried to catch my breath! I was panting heavily, still trying to figure out how all this could be happening.

Suddenly, I could feel the change in the air. Every hair on my body and on my head stood straight up as if I were touching an electric Tesla ball.

The next thing I heard was a voice. The voice was a booming voice like thunder I had never heard. It was so incredibly loud that I thought that the whole world could hear Him speak.

The lady in the next bed didn't even stir. The voice said, "I AM NEVER TOO LATE."

Then came a sound like a loud ticking clock that seemed to shoot across the ceiling right over me...and in its wake, a brilliant bright light shone down on me from above.

The sound came again and crossed over the existing beam of bright light. It, too, filled the room with the same brilliant bright light and formed the shape of a cross right over my bed.

I tried repeatedly to wake my roommate friend by screaming, "Lady, lady, wake up. You gotta see this!"

I couldn't get a witness of the "Greatest Show On Earth" and it was no circus.

I knew that I had just had a holy encounter with my Great and Glorious God! I was so elated by His presence that I threw my arms in the air to worship God like never before. Humbled and awed that He had given me audience in my hospital room, I threw Him kisses, talked with Him and prayed, imagining that I was before His throne for what seemed like hours before I was exhausted and fell asleep.

Just as they had promised, my husband and the two nurses woke me early the next morning. I saw the soft rays of the rising sun slip over both beds reminding me that I was still in the hospital. The two nurses, close to the end of their shifts, went to get the doctor in case they needed to help him with the D&C.

I was glad to have a moment alone with my husband but concerned and scared that he wouldn't believe my story. Instead he sat on my bed and held me tight in his arms and said to me that he believed every word. It was a rush of relief that his love for me would keep him from escorting me off in a shiny wheelchair to the psych ward the next floor down.

The doctor arrived next to examine me. He was thorough. He said that during the night, I had naturally finished miscarrying any fetal tissue and that it would no longer be necessary to have a D&C.

He spoke to us about special counseling that was available to young couples like us who go through this. He said he would do the paperwork to release us from the hospital and that I should be fine with plenty of rest and special care from my husband for the next week or so.

We left the room passing by the lady in bed number one, still deep in slumber. I remember thinking that someone should check to see if she was still breathing.

The elevator was a quiet ride down to the first floor as my mind juggled all that was said and had happened. Still, I struggled believing that my husband might think he married a "nut job," and that he didn't sign up for this. Instead, he kissed my forehead and gently helped me into the car, assuaging all my fears.

The what's and the why's went unanswered as the days passed by, but we held tight to our faith that God had a holy plan that someday He would unveil. Still, my physical body was sore from the medical prodding and the miscarriage.

Our hearts and minds were still saddened by the loss of our child. So we decided not to try to get pregnant for a while because we both needed time to heal.

We shared and talked about our good God, His son Jesus, and the Holy Spirit, and read everything we could find devouring book after book like *Mama's Home Cookin.*

Just about three weeks later, my husband wanted to go up our favorite mountain trail. He told me to get dressed for a fun but easy hike. I agreed, and rushed to put on my favorite hiking shorts, which wouldn't zip up. I tussled with the zipper but found that my tummy was still swollen. We stared at each other with puzzling looks, reverting back to the same mind-juggling that we had experienced three weeks earlier in the hospital elevator.

"No, it couldn't be," we thought. Or "could it be a tumor? So right away we called my regular OB/GYN to make an appointment. She scheduled us just days later. After her examination she left the room for a while, and we wondered if we should tell her of our ordeal three weeks earlier.

When she returned, she had a smile and news that we were three and a half months pregnant.

Two gigantic, mind-blowing things happened just then. First, we wondered if God could have returned to us our baby that death tried to destroy? Or second, we thought "There's no way on earth we were going to tell her that I had just had a miscarriage three weeks ago." IF we did tell her, she would for sure slip both of us a medicinal mickey and we would awaken in some asylum south of the city.

Needless to say, we were in shock and awe at the greatest of news. The why's started to be answered. Why? Because God is great and merciful! Why? Because God answers prayer! Why? Because

He had a plan and a future and a sure destiny for the child in my womb and death would have no victory! The questions to the "whys" were falling like dominoes on display.

The answer to the questions of what happened in that hospital room with the wind, and where it came from, went unanswered until much later.

We started making more and more frequent visits to the doctor just to revel in God's gift and to hear the baby's little rapid heart beat. Then the day came that the doctor told us that we could see our baby by ultrasound and that we could be privy to the sex of our baby. We declined only so that we could someday soon open another surprise gift from God. One day closer to my seventh month, I told my husband that I thought the baby would be a little girl.

"How do you know?" he asked?

"I just have a feeling," I retorted.

It was time to make ready the nursery, so we bought little bunny wallpaper and long lacy curtains that hung down from the ceiling to flank each side of the handmade cradle that my husband's father built in joyous anticipation of his new grandchild. It was perfect!

Then we brought in the rest of the furniture: a changing table, a diaper pail, and an old rocking chair that clicked after each rock. There was one last thing daddy wanted to paint on the still empty wall. He gathered his paint colors and escorted me out so he could create a work of art. A work of art it was!

He had painted a huge wall-sized rainbow of many beautiful colors that stretched from wall to wall dotted with two butterflies.

We were ready for our baby!

Two months later, exactly nine months from the baby's original due date, Jesse was born. We hired a midwife to deliver the baby in her unconventional birthing room with a stand-alone tub of warm water and a fire flickering in the corner, bathing the room in a soft orange light.

We were alone with only the midwife and a registered nurse who happened to be my dearest and closest friend from childhood.

It was late evening on Valentine's Day, and I pushed hard to have Jesse's birthday synonymous with that celebration. Finally early, very early the next morning, Jesse made a debut. But Jesse *wasn't* a girl! He was born eyes open without a whimper. He looked around the room and then locked his sights on his daddy.

They placed Jesse in his daddy's arms first, and then after they cut the umbilical cord they placed him in mine. Still, with never a cry, he seemed to study this new environment like he was taking mental notes.

Jesse grew strong and fast and was a perfect baby! He never had colic, he awoke only once a night for feeding, and he wasn't much of a crier. We often would tell him of his story when he was little so that he would know from early childhood that "God had a specific destiny planned for him." Many times after he could talk, he would interrupt my conversations with friends and insist that I tell them Jesse's story.

He has grown through the years with a strong resolve of who he is and a stronger constitution of Christ in him. He is always kind and loving to others. He decided that his city was in peril and needed change. He became a police officer so that he could be that change. He is a preacher's kid and an incredible musician and songwriter. Jesse married his beautiful childhood girlfriend and now has two beautiful babies. He's an example of Jesus's love both at work and in his private life. Jesse's story is not over....neither is mine.

Years ago as I was thinking and pondering the goodness of God, my thoughts went back to that night in the hospital room. I remembered that I had never understood the tornado wind in my room that night. So I asked God what it was. And this time instead of a loud booming voice that shook me, I heard, like a kiss, His soft and gentle whisper in my ear, "That wasn't a room tornado—that was my breath!"

8

CHAPTER

MOUNTAINTOP RETREAT

SHORTLY AFTER OUR EPIC HOSPITAL visitation with baby Jesse, my husband and I decided to take a short, three-day retreat to the beautiful mountain peaks just north of Santa Fe. We took with us one bottle of inexpensive sweet red wine and a box of cheese crackers (for communion), enough water for three days, our Bibles, the dog, and our camping gear.

The highest peak was our target, so we drove on seldom-used roads that slowly turned into skinny cow paths. Still not sure where we were going, my husband stopped the truck and prayed a prayer of guidance and safety. Continuing on, he suddenly made a sharp left turn off the path onto very bumpy terrain.

"Where are we going?" I asked.

Without saying a word he pointed to three ponderosa pines that stood off in the distance. As we drew near, we found the three trees in a triangle surrounding a shiny new campsite.

The stones for the fire were fresh and newly laid, not sooty like old or used campsites. In the middle of the stones, wood was meticulously placed teepee style. A very neat pile of enough wood for three days was stacked off to the side with no tire or foot tracks anywhere to be found.

It seemed as though someone had come to prepare a three-day retreat for us. Some would say that it could have been a boy scout, but we were convinced that this was more of a personal invitation.

My husband said that he felt we were to string our tent between the three trees, so we did. We then settled into our outdoor environment. After a quick inspection tour of the area, we sat on a fallen log to take in the majestic scape that wrapped around our camp. The crisp air and a cool breeze brought a refreshing sense of God's presence. We sat in silence to hear the whisper sounds of the mountaintop...His Voice.

Not long into our quietude, a swarm of pesky flies and mountain bees flew around us, curious of who had invaded their hood. After much swatting and slapping, I grew frustrated and tried to run to the tent for a short respite but my husband wouldn't have it. He reminded me that Scripture teaches us that we have been given power and authority over the pestilence of the earth. So instead of retreating, we stirred up our hearts filled with His faith and started commanding the flies and bees to leave this area.

In just seconds the buzzing and humming irritants left. As fast as they had appeared, they were gone and stayed gone the entire three day retreat.

Then from a distance, we heard a sound that I had never heard before. It sounded like far off bugles getting louder and louder. Just behind our camp down a small hill, a huge herd of majestic elk was gathering as if to greet us. They were bugling, bugling as if they were performing a Hallelujah Handel's opus. What a tremendous sight to see so many elk so close to us.

We had planned a three-day fast with only communion wine and cheese crackers to sustain us. So we prepared our communion meal, read from our bibles, and sat in silent meditation.

We noticed the sun slip behind a cloud but failed to notice the dark nimbus clouds slowly sneaking up all around us.

In the afternoon, it started turning darker and darker on our mountaintop.

It started with a soft drizzle, so we scrambled to get our scattered possessions and our dog into the safety of our tent. It was just in time, too, because it started raining pretty hard. I almost made it to my tent when my husband, standing in the falling rain, reminded me that we also have the authority over the elements of the earth. With our certitude faith, we started speaking to the rain to stop.

What happened next was hilarious! The clouds over us opened up and dumped buckets of drenching rain soaking our hair, clothes and shoes. We didn't move; instead we started laughing. Laughing so loud and hard at the scene that each of us were beholding. We looked like drowned rats and then our hilarity turned into belly laughter. Still we didn't budge but something started to happen.

The rain suddenly stopped and the clouds started peeling back in what became a perfect circle about a quarter mile radius right above our camp. The rays of the afternoon sun bathed our campsite with sunshine and drying warmth as the thunderstorm continued to storm all around us.

For the remainder of our time on the mountaintop, it continued to storm except the circle of sky above us that stayed warm with sunlight during the day and starry heavens at night.

The afternoon of the third day, we packed up our gear and the dog and headed home filled with Psalm136:1-9. We came to the mountaintop to find God but what we found was that He had already been waiting for us.

9

EVER LIVIN'
CAR TROUBLE

I WAS ON MY WAY TO AN APPOINTMENT downtown, in the middle lane on a busy highway, when the front struts of my car blew a brand new tire on the passenger side.

Grateful that I maintained control, I barely got the car over to the inside emergency lane. At 65 MPH, it was a harried struggle, but I managed to pull the car out of the way of the heavy traffic and come to a stop.

I stayed in the car to gather my wits and could feel the car shake with every passing vehicle matching the speed of my racing heart.

I mouthed a simple prayer, "Jesus, help me!"

Before I even finished my prayer, my phone beeped with a text from my son Jesse asking if I wanted to join him for lunch.

"Yes," I replied but I'm stuck on the freeway with a blown tire. After getting my GPS whereabouts, he said he would be right there to help me. I was so relieved that my prayer was so quickly answered.

Oh, and did I mention that *he* was a police officer? In a very short amount of time, he drove up behind me in his off-duty truck. He hugged me and told me to sit in his truck while he changed the tire. He struggled to remove the lug nuts, but failed because of the recent work done on the struts. He called for a special truck to aid and assist. Less then five minutes passed, when a huge yellow transformer-lookin' truck pulled up behind my son's truck with a huge flashing arrow to detour the traffic from the left lane. A big burly guy with special tools helped my son remove the wheel and replace it with the little spare from my trunk. On inspection, the spare needed air because it was nearly flat.

Just then the phone rang again and it was my other son David that asked, "Momma, is that you stuck on the freeway? And is that my brother behind you?"

"Yes," I explained and told him what had just transpired. He said that he was turning around and would be right there. Sure enough, in only moments my other son, David, pulled up in front of the three of us in his truck. Oh, did I mention that he was a fire fighter? By the time that my fire fighter son drove up on the scene, we were discussing how in the heck all of us were going to be able to pick up enough speed to re-enter the fast-paced right lanes.

So my police officer son settled me back in my car with the leaky spare and said that I needed to follow the truck in front while he drives behind me.

Then there was a loud honk. It was the huge yellow truck telling all of us to pull in front of him so that he could detour the traffic from lane-to-lane as he escorted us to the nearest exit. So with all of our emergency lights flashing we finally exited the freeway but stayed in convoy formation all the way to the tire store. With my fire fighter son in front and my police officer son guarding my back, I felt like royalty being escorted to safety by The City's Finest!

After reaching the tire store and making the car repair arrangements, the man behind the counter said that it would take about an hour-and-a-half. So I turned and asked my boys if I could take them to lunch. They took me up on the invitation and we went to a nice restaurant close by.

I just sat and listened as they "talked trash" (colloquialism, meaning teasing) about their chosen vocations. Then it changed to sports and their favorite season draft picks. I just enjoyed listening to the chatter and started thinking how very blessed I was to have them rescue me and then to share this time with them. Though their lives are very busy, I had them all to myself. So what the devil intended for a nasty day, God faithfully turned to be a day of great and many sweet blessings on my road through life.

10

"HOLY SMOKE"

When all has been heard, the end of the matter is: fear God [Worship Him with awe-filled reverence, knowing that He is almighty God] and keep His love commandments, for this is the whole of man, the full original purpose of His creation, the object of God's providence, the root of character, the foundation of all happiness, the adjustment to all inharmonious circumstances and conditions under the sun and the whole duty of every man. —Eccl. 12:13 Amp

IN 1985 WE WERE JUST A YOUNG MINISTRY, a seven-member band for Jesus. We found, in the Word that in Isaiah 6:4, that it speaks of the temple being "filled with smoke." So we decided we wanted to *be that very smoke that cloaked His presence*—so we named our ministry "Holy Smoke."

Holy Smoke ministered in church services, park outreaches, and concert venues so that we could deliver the good message that "God, Jesus, and the Holy Spirit were lovers of man and not punitive judges ready to punish mans sinfulness," We were always hopeful that our worship and messages stirred the lost and the indifferent to ask questions about this Jesus—the very Jesus who knew and understood the burden of being human and the Jesus who turned his hostility in the temple toward empty religion and yet His mercy always turned to the outcasts and sinner.

God has always desired to live in His people. He is Love, and He never desired to live in temples made with human hands. He wanted to dwell in our hearts. Now, because of Jesus, He has finally found a home in which to live–a home made of living stones.

In essence, our vision for Holy Smoke was to bring His presence and glory to be *seen* in the world when we come together with the singular purpose of praising and worshiping Him as one people.

And, that then His Glory will fill the earth—His own promise to us is that "if He be lifted up, He will draw all men unto Himself.

Man was created to be a worshiper. It is in our DNA. Man's choice is not whether or not he will worship, it is only whom or what he will worship Our purpose as His people is to flood the atmosphere with His manifest glory and presence. The world groans for the revelation of the son's of God. It has been said that the chief principle of worship is this: "Whatever we worship, we will end up serving. The more we worship something, the more we become like the thing we worship."

In 2001 we were called to pastor and build Worldwide Worship Center, a place where we can all come together to worship in unrestrained, full-out love and praise for Him 24/7. A place for continual worship just as it was in David's day.

For thirty some years, God's glory was seen over Jerusalem. During that time, there was no sickness, no wars, but great prosperity and the visible glory that even unbelievers recognized the dwelling presence of God.

Though our services are still small, those that come are faithful and anointed ministers—disciples, not just church members. We have never given up hope that we will someday build our own building to house this *big vision* that He has placed in our hearts. Through the years we have ministered the Word and Worship in churches of all denominations throughout the United States, Eastern Europe, the West Indies, South America, and Cuba. I could fill volumes of all the incredible stories that we have witnessed but here are just a few to hopefully pique your curiosity.

JAMAICA

"And I, if I am lifted up from the earth, I will draw all peoples unto Myself." —John 12:32

WE GET TEASED WHEN PEOPLE HEAR that we have ministered in Jamaica. They say things like, "Oh you were suffering for Jesus, right?" These are the very people who have never been to the inner-cities filled with poverty close to third-world status. Most indigenous people don't frolic on the sunny beaches of Jamaica. They may have jobs in some of the beach front hotels for the lucky, but most live their entire lives within their poverty-stricken boundaries.

We landed at the airport Friday afternoon and were immediately asked to do a concert that evening for the inner city youth. We were escorted on to a vacant lot where the people started building a stage for us out of the wood pallets that they could find. Very impressed with their ingenuity, I noticed the neighborhood families starting to gather around the make-shift stage to listen to this "Holy Smoke " from America. About 300 ft. away we noticed two angry men with very red eyes, smoking these huge rolls of ganja, trying to stare us down as if to tell us, "oh, we'll show you holy smoke!"

We always started with worship, and then came the message from my husband that they were deeply loved, cherished people with purpose and God given destinies. He told them that worshiping God would change the spiritual landscape of their city as they continued to invite the presence of the Holy Spirit. When we finished, we invited all who would come to the front so we could pray with them.

The two angry men stood up and started coming towards the front, dropped to their knees, and asked for prayer. As we prayed with them their eyes started to clear from red to runny with tears of jubilation that they had met with God.

Back in the states a few months later, we got a letter from one of those two men telling us that they were now both ministers of Jesus Christ, ministering to the same people about the glory and the presence of God that was changing the atmosphere of their little town.

Another move of God came when we were scheduled to preach at a very religious and very strict denominational church in the inner-city early Sunday morning. We were kindly greeted by the Pastor but not so much by the four elders of the church who looked at us with icy skepticism and sat back in their row of fancy chairs.

Worship was glorious and the message that my husband was led to share was called, "Religion Stinks!" Expecting to be quickly escorted out of the church I was not prepared for what happened next. My husband spoke a Word over the Pastor about the strong presence of the Holy Spirit wanting to move in this church:

It started with the pastor falling to his knees in sobbing sweet surrender to whatever the Holy Spirit would lead. Then all the women of the church stood and started waving their kerchiefs in solidarity, singing and dancing until all the pews in there rigid rows were pushed helter skelter to make room for now the men and children to partake of this holy gala affair.

There came a sound of soft singing that soon exploded like the Philharmonic Orchestra into heavenly songs that resonated the rafters that continued for what seemed like hours.

No one cared, as we were all swept up in a heavenly quantum, lost in His presence except for a still rigid conspicuous row of four angry elders with their arms folded in their fancy chairs.

Hours later in happy, holy exhaustion we started to pack up when we noticed a low rumble of voices slowly rising in frustration and volume.

It was the pastor trying to explain to the elders that what had just happened was answer to his desperate prayer to God for more of His presence.

They just couldn't see it so they fired the pastor that day. Still filled with great joy and the Holy Spirit, he quickly called a friend pastor across town to borrow his friends church so they could have services next week over there. It had been told to us that they had glorious Holy Spirit church the very next Sunday with his entire congregation attending. Sadly, the only ones who didn't show were the four elders that didn't have a congregation to preach to, not even one.

ROMANIA

And may the Lord make you increase and abound in love to one another... —1 Thessalonians 3:12

OUR FIRST TRIP TO TIMISOARA, ROMANIA was an eye-opener to the world of evil, controlling despots that rule God's people with dark deceit and malice. One year earlier, Nicolae Ceausescu was the communist leader of Romania, considered one of the most repressive in all Eastern Europe. Tried and found guilty of mass genocide and economic sabotage, he, with his wife, were executed by firing squad on December 25th, 1989.

Christians were among the many whose human rights suffered severe abuse. Bibles were confiscated and turned into toilet paper. His secret police, the Securitate, would arrest Christians who hid pages of Scripture in the drywall or hems of curtains in their homes. Ceausescu, was brutal to his own people causing severe repression, and the harshest methods of punishment in the world.

After settling in our hotel, we were escorted to the first scheduled prison visit since Ceausescu, there in Timisoara. Walking up to the huge iron gates that loomed before us was quite intimidating. Each of us carried music equipment in as the huge iron gates shut tight behind us with a resounding clang shutting us in. We were led to a small room with a rustic green door and told to sit as they summoned the warden. He entered the small room with his big stature of a man, six foot and probably 275 pounds. With our translator and the warden in Romanian discourse, he turned to explain the do's and the don'ts.

Again we were escorted to another much bigger but dark and dingy room with bunches of dilapidated chairs and told to set up towards the front of the windowless, barn-like room. The wretched smell in the room was so pungent and disgusting that I had to talk myself into not spewing the contents of my stomach.

Not prepared at all to witness the sight I next beheld, I stood with eyes huge and a gaping mouth at the rows of men led into the room by the guards. Men bent over with the burden of heavy chains and iron balls that rolled and clanged with each step. Prison uniforms that mostly were just filthy rags that imitated the black and white stripes that you would see at costume parties or some old cartoons. Unkempt, unshowered, unshaven, underfed, and unhealthy eyes stared back at us through what seemed a veil of hopelessness that saturated the dark, dank room along with an even more intense, wretched stench.

It was so hard to look back at these men thinking that most of them were just political prisoners, still stuck in the red tape of the previous administration; bold and courageous men that led revolts against the tyranny to protect their families and those they loved; thieves that were caught stealing bread, cheese or fruit only to feed their starving babies.

We started singing our worshipful songs to invite the Holy Spirit to flood this room with His presence. All the songs were in English, so we had to rely on the anointing to translate the heart message we were trying to convey. One of our songs had a "Hallelujah" chorus that quickly became one of the most beautiful and anointed Christian songs that I had ever heard. Every one of the prisoners knew that universal word, "Hallelujah."

Seemingly, now unencumbered by their chains, they stood with raised hands and hearts joining in one voice that welcomed in the Holy Spirit. A holy light bathed the room removing any trace of that wretched stench and the gloom of hopelessness that earlier had filled that room. Still standing, still singing, every man shone from their face a brightness that must have come from somewhere deep within them, melding with the holy aurora that was transforming every man in that room.

Even the guards seemed to want to be a part but nervously looked toward the warden who now had closed his eyes and bowed his head. "Hallelujah" after "Hallelujah," we continued on as there was no tick of the clock or time-zone that could interrupt this open-heaven.

Suddenly, it seemed like a whole other hosts of voices joined in with ours reaching decibels too high for humans to reach. Now united together, heaven and earth, we continued singing "Hallelujah" to bring glory and honor to the One True Living God. Suddenly, there fell a holy hush. As if someone turned the volume button to "off." There was no sound to be heard. Only a feeling of cleansing breath that seemed to wash over everyone in the room.

Now the warden signaled to the guards to ready their prisoners to return to their cells but graciously allowed us to individually shake hands and love on these men who had just been saturated in the Holy Spirit. Gently kissing our hands and mouthing goodbye they exited through the iron doors. Now back in the small room with the green door, we asked the warden, through our translator, if we could leave Bibles written in Romanian to leave for the prisoners. Unexpectedly fast he replied yes and asked if he could have some to give away to the families in the neighborhood. We had plenty so we left him with a healthy stash. On our way out of the prison after piling up the van with equipment and team passengers, We drove by a house with the warden, brimming with Bibles, passing each one out just as he had promised. Only God!

We witnessed so many other moves of God's Glory in Cluj Napoka, Tigru Mures, Timisoara, orphanages, public schools, churches, another national prison, and ministry outreaches to the hungry and needy throughout most all of Romania that I will someday write about in another book.

The people of Romania are heroes to me. A courageous people, who in the face of gunfire, turned an entire national army over to the side of human decency and righteousness. A people with the Securitate threat of imprisonment and torture never ceased to be faithful to God and share his unchanging Love to those who would hear.

Forging so many lasting friendships throughout Romania, we returned several times and hope to one day return again. My husband penned this song in honor of the brave and persistent peoples that brought about such enormous change to their country. This song was translated by a dear Romanian friend and we sung it as an anthem many times in Romania.

Words and music by Stacy McDermott, BMI

There is a light that shining through the darkness of Romania.
There is a hand that's guiding all the lion-hearted saints of God
Who've risked their lives to live His Word assured He will prevail
To fight the unrelenting foe and cry "we shall not fail."

There is a light.
There is a Truth that's living, it's growing stronger in Romania.
There is a hand that's giving of His Grace a never ending flow.
That hope and truth and love may grow all sheltered
'neath His name.
And should the darkness come again the saints will cry, "we fight again."

There is a light, there is a light that's shining brighter than the day
There is a Truth, there is a truth that Christ is coming back someday
There is a trust and we will put our trust in Jesus as the way for us to
Overcome the darkness in Romania

There are a people hungering for a spiritual awakening.
They are a people praying for revival in their broken land
And strengthened by the Masters' hand their shout is "victory"
Foul Satan is defeated, we'll preach Christ triumphantly!
There is a light
There is a freedom rising through the blood of those who've laid down
their lives
They are the saints whose dying has lit the fire that is not quenched
And burns away the evil stench of man's prideful regime
Their hope remains their call is strong, "come live the Master's dream!"
There is a light
Victory! Though the battle rages Victory! Till the war is won
Victory Hail the Rock of Ages, Victory through the risen son

GUYANA

*For God so loved the world that He gave His only begotten Son... —*John 3:16

ON OUR SECOND TRIP TO GUYANA, we arrived at the airport to find out that because of some recent civil unrest, the President of Guyana sent his personal car and driver to pick us up and take us to our hotel. As the flags of Guyana fluttered on each side of the front engine, it was surreal that we were riding in the President's car, even though it was 2 o'clock in the morning with zero fanfare. It was still a great privilege to be invited by the President to minister the Good News of Jesus to his people here in his country.

We had an invitation to minister at the evening festival/market that they had every week. There were vendors of all kinds: food, trinkets, treasures, and even local folk art.

The atmosphere was festive with live musicians and spots of dancing. Always praying that our worship and then message in the Word never became "usual to us but remain usable by the Holy Spirit," we again asked the people to come up if they wanted prayer.

Somewhere from the middle of the huge crowd, they parted to let through this very skinny man, clothed only in a black trash bag covering his loins. He made his way to the front and my husband asked him what we could pray for him about.

The man told us how the doctors said that he had fourth-stage cancer and that there was no more that they could do. He wore the garbage bag because he no longer was able to control his bowels and it was easier to change bags than clothes.

With no hope and only days to live, he made his way to pray. My husband hugged him with a holy hug and in his ear told him how greatly cherished he was by God. He told him that God said that healing was His children's bread and asked him if he would trust God to heal him.

Then with bowed heads, my husband prayed a simple faith prayer, hugged him again then shook his hand. He hurried off into the same crowd from where he came.

Next evening, when we were setting up again to minister in the same market, a man rushed with excitement over to us. He was wearing a crisp ironed shirt and pants, shined shoes and socks, was freshly showered and with a smile that matched his countenance.

It was hard to tell that he was the *same man that just last night had asked for prayer wearing a garbage bag.* He testified that when he prayed with us last night to this unfamiliar and unseen God, with child-like faith, he believed that because God loved him, God would heal him. He didn't slip away last night because of a still abiding hopelessness, but he sensed a surge of healing love that totally washed over him.

His doctors, that morning, *were perplexed yet confirmed that they could no longer find any trace of cancer.* He was transformed into a new man, body soul and spirit.

Still in Guyana but deep in the jungle forest, in a little tiny village, Holy Smoke was ministering and sharing Jesus' love for them.

When we had packed up and started the car, I noticed a little boy scurry down a ladder that was attached to his hut on stilts. He ran next to the car, racing to wave goodbye to us. His little tummy extended, wearing a dirty loin cloth, he smiled so big at me that I said out loud that I wanted to steal him, take him home and raise him as a strong Christian young man. Just then, I heard a strong but gentle rebuke from God. He said that the little boy didn't need my pity filled with prejudices and judgments. He said that the little boy was *right where He wanted him and that he was very happy and that He would watch over him.*

Duh! A hard lesson to learn but one that unfortunately my pride would allow me to repeat twice more on my pilgrimage through life.

THE DOMINICAN REPUBLIC

The Spirit Himself bears witness with our spirit, that we are the children of God. —Romans 8:16

Never before had we witnessed a move of God so strong like we did in the streets of Santa Domingo. Holy Smoke, ever ready to sow the Word of God in every nation and land, we were pleasantly surprised that this time *we* would be the reapers. *'One sows and another reaps. I sent you to reap that for which you have not labored; others have labored and you have entered into their labor.'* John 4: 37, 38. It was just like we had gone on a swanky vacation and landed on heavenly shores because when we asked if they wanted to know Jesus, their swift and sure answer was "yes" and "could you pray for me now?"

As we are setting up at the outdoor Market/Festival, we noticed two very young prostitutes walking on the other side of the street. Embolden by His strong presence, we asked the girls if they knew Jesus and if they wanted prayer. They both swiftly agreed but one of them slipped to her knees, eyes filling with tears, she said that her father was a preacher and that she needed Jesus in her life. Right there we started praying for her and encouraged her that her sins had been forgiven and that right now, she was a cherished work of art to God. As we continued encouraging them, a john drove up looking to hire them for the evening but they were locked into the Divine Love that was bathing them— so they waved him off.

Now under the influence of unconditional Love, they followed us over to the Festival. Still setting up, two local police men came up to me and asked me if we had a license to play music here. Caught of guard, I said "No, but do you know Jesus?"

He said, "I do but he doesn't," pointing to his partner.

So after sharing with them both about God's goodness and what we were doing there, they ignored their own statute and proceeded to hand out flyers and bibles to the passing crowds for us.

A sad young woman who was meandering at the fountain had no shoes. A friend on our team removed her own shoes and gave them to her. They were perfect fit! Still having a sad face, I asked what was the matter.

She looked at me teary-eyed and said that my God couldn't love her. I asked why she believed that and she said, "Because I am gay and He won't accept me."

I told her that for sure He would accept her and shower her in His Love for He knows very well the fragile constitution of the human spirit. I told her how much He wants to bathe us in His perfect and Divine Love accepting all who would come to Him. She remained with us all night enjoying His Holy Presence.

Every single person that I spoke with the entire time on the Island either already knew Him or wanted to know Him and joined in the reveling of His Glory supernaturally saturating the Island.

Late that night as we went back to our hotel for food and rest the maitre d', not knowing who we were or what we did, asked if he could sing us a song that he remembered from his childhood.

We enthusiastically replied "Yes!"

He began to sing with certitude about the God that he knew and loved as a child. After singing his song, he disappeared into the kitchen returning with every waiter and cook and employee there, having them each give testimony or song to the glory of God. I hated leaving Santa Domingo because I didn't want to miss what God was doing on His beloved Island.

Weeks later, He gave me an incredible dream about Santa Domingo that I will share at another time.

There are still so many places like Ireland, Germany, and Cuba that I have been witness to the Divine Passion that God has for His people worldwide.

This faith journey that has spanned the decades of my life is not yet over. I am still walking this love road following its curves and straightways. Learning to love everyone I meet. I could tell more but this will suffice to say that God still moves today in visions, dreams and supernatural manifestations.

Do not "seek" a vision or holy manifestation, but instead *seek the face of God through Jesus and the Holy Spirit* and He will light up your life with His Divine Presence to overflowing!

HOLY SMOKE MINISTRIES
CDs are Available on iTunes

KK Mac is a singer, songwriter, and author.
Her CD *On Tour Across the Heavens* will bless and
transport you into the presence of God!

Heavy Timber is a beautiful and anointed
Holy Smoke Ministries Album.
All of the songs were written by Stacy McDermott.
Their ministry has excited audiences worldwide!

Contact the ministry
for music and speaking engagments:
Email: Chatwithkaykaymac@gmail.com

www.ingramcontent.com/pod-product-compliance
Lightning Source LLC
Chambersburg PA
CBHW071018040426
42443CB00007B/836